Writing

DEVELOPING ADULT TEACHING AND LEARNING: PRACTITIONER GUIDES

Sue Grief and Jan Chatterton

promoting adult learning

(England and Wales)
21 De Montfort Street
Leicester LE1 7GE

Company registration no. 2603322
Charity registration no. 1002775
Published by NIACE in association with NRDC.

NIACE has a broad remit to promote lifelong learning opportunities for adults.
NIACE works to develop increased participation in education and training,
particularly for those who do not have easy access because of class, gender, age,
race, language and culture, learning difficulties or disabilities, or insufficient
financial resources.

For a full catalogue of all NIACE's publications visit
www.niace.org.uk/publications

Cataloguing in Publications Data
A CIP record for this title is available from the British Library
ISBN 978-1-86201-335-3

Cover design by Creative by Design Limited, Paisley
Designed and typeset by Creative by Design Limited, Paisley
Printed and bound by Aspect Binders and Print Ltd

Developing adult teaching and learning: Practitioner guides

This is one of several linked publications arising from the five Effective Practice Studies carried out by the National Research and Development Centre for Adult Literacy and Numeracy (NRDC) from 2003 to 2007.

The five studies explored effective teaching and learning in reading, writing, numeracy, ESOL and using ICT. To date, three series of publications have been produced from the Effective Practice Studies: the research reports and the development project reports, all published by NRDC; and these practitioner guides, published in partnership between NIACE and NRDC.

For more information on the first two series, please see **www.nrdc.org.uk**

Contents

Acknowledgements

The authors would like to thank the following people for their contribution to this publication.

Monica Collingham who recruited and supported the practitioners in South Yorkshire and London, and who contributed to the publication in many ways.

The practitioners who worked with us to shape the publication and who provided feedback on drafts and contributed suggestions, examples and quotations:

- Catherine Bennett
- Linda Gatti
- John Parkinson
- Bronwen Ray
- Kate Roberts
- Kath Swinney
- Jane Tones

The practitioners who worked on the project on collaborative writing and shared their findings and materials:

- Alison Bagshaw
- Jean Brunwin
- Sue Chatwood
- Fay Middleton
- Ruth North
- Bronwen Ray
- Marina Richards
- Jane Tones

The writing frame on page 16 is reproduced from a communication course developed by Kath Swinney and Iain Jackson for Sheffield ACL, Cite-e-net.

Peer review

This guide was peer reviewed. The critical readers were:

- Judith Gawn, NIACE
- Nora Hughes, Institute of Education
- Gay Lobley, Consultant

About this book

This book:

- has been written for teachers working with adults and young people in *Skills for Life* provision;

- starts from the findings of a research study on writing undertaken by the NRDC, *Effective Teaching and Learning: Writing* (Grief, Meyer and Burgess 2007). It also draws on a previous NRDC study which included reviews of research and of practice in the teaching of writing (Kelly, Soundranayagam and Grief 2004) and a more recent small-scale project exploring collaborative writing (for simplicity we refer to the 'research project' and the 'review');

- is relevant to what happens in the classroom or other teaching context. We have attempted to unpick the implications of the research findings in a very practical way;

- has been written by practitioners and researchers working together. Two groups of practitioners have commented on the findings of the research projects and have advised on the structure and content of the book. They have also provided a range of ideas and examples to illustrate and extend the messages from the research;

- is not a manual on how to teach writing. It is intended to encourage the reader to reflect on writing and the ways in which they teach this in their classes, to provide examples and to inspire them to try new approaches;

- does not cover all aspects of teaching writing. It begins from the research study and develops a number of themes. Suggestions for further reading are included at the end of each section; and

- challenges readers to ask questions and undertake their own classroom research in order to understand better how best to help their learners develop as writers.

The key messages in the book are relevant to all teaching contexts. The examples included within the book are deliberately drawn from a wide range of teaching contexts and from classes at different levels, but teachers will need to explore for themselves how best they can be applied in the particular contexts in which they teach.

Readers who are interested to learn more about the nature of the research and the findings are encouraged to read the NRDC summary report *Effective Approaches to the Teaching and Learning of Writing* (Grief, Kelly and Soundranayagam, 2004).

1 | Writing matters

'The standard of literacy shown by people filling in the double-sided application form... is often very poor... Many applicants can't construct a sentence.'
(CBI, 2006, p. 9)

'For me, writing is healing, it is also communicating. But above all, it's powerful....

Writing is powerful. It gets across ideas. And there is always the chance that you might reach someone.'

Meiling Jin in the introduction to her poetry *Gifts from my Grandmother* (1986)

Saturday 20 June 1942

I haven't written for a few days, because I wanted first of all to think about my diary; not only because I have never done so before, because it seems to me that neither I - nor for that matter anyone else - will be interested in the unbosomings of a thirteen year old. Still what does that matter? I want to write, but more than that, I want to bring out all kinds of things that lie buried in my heart...
(*Diary of Anne Frank*)

I declare that all the above is correct

Name: John Smith

Signed: *John Smith*

The situation is severe and has required us to take some difficult decisions which will have implications for us all. I believe it is important that I explain these to you in person and am therefore asking all staff to attend a meeting in the large meeting room at 12.00 noon today.

Alrite Matt! Do u want to meet 4a couple of drinks after wrk? Wud b gud 2 cu. Any ideas where 2 go? x Stace

These examples remind us that:

- writing is about communication;
- power can be exercised through writing;
- we use writing to express our personality and our emotions;
- writing can help us discover more about ourselves;
- writing can help us reflect on and sort out ideas and experiences;
- we write for a specific audience and for a purpose;
- new technologies do not mean that we write less; and
- we make judgements about people on the basis of their writing.

These are all reasons for making sure that writing, in a range of forms and for a range of purposes, figures large in literacy classes.

Writing is important to learners

Anyone who regularly interviews new adult learners will know that wanting to improve their writing is very frequently a motivating factor when deciding to join a course. Figures from a recent NRDC study of adults born in 1970 indicated that 25 per cent of the adults interviewed reported some problems with writing compared to 8 per cent reporting problems with reading (Bynner and Parsons, 2006).

Learning to write or gaining confidence as a writer can be empowering. As the quotation below illustrates, it can change lives:

> *Before, I could never fill in forms. They may as well have been written in another language. In the end I didn't even look at them. I asked my sister to fill them in for me and I just signed them. Now I was beginning to fill in forms on my own. I began to help my children with their homework, something I could never do before. As I improved, so did their results at school. Going back to education was changing all our lives. History was not going to repeat itself, I was making sure of that...*
> *Returning to education to learn to read and write, was one of the most frightening things I have done, but it was also one of the best.* (Marie McNamara, from her book *Getting Better*, 2007)

Writing is important to employers

A recent report from the Confederation of British Industry (CBI) highlights the importance of writing and underlines the value employers place on writing:

> *Reading and writing must be considered separately. They tend to be rolled up together and treated as one, but writing tends to pose much more of a problem. The ability to put together a piece of writing that conveys meaning clearly and accurately is an essential functional skill. The inability to put together a short coherent piece of writing has serious implications for those seeking work or thinking of changing jobs.* (CBI, 2006)

Writing needs to be placed in the spotlight

Reading and writing with adult learners are very often linked under the heading of 'literacy'. There is no doubt that two are closely related and exploration of the ways in which the learning of one supports the other in adult literacy classes would be of great interest. However, the danger of thinking only in terms of 'literacy' is that we don't give sufficient attention to either skill or to the distinct strategies that teachers need to use in teaching them. The research study demonstrated that there is real value to be gained by placing the spotlight on writing and in this book we encourage teachers to do just this.

2 | Moving from research to practice

The research study

The aim of the Effective Practice Study on writing was to explore the links between teachers' practice in the teaching of writing and learners' progress in writing.

The study involved a total of 341 learners in 49 classes from a wide range of *Skills for Life* provision. We observed three full sessions in each class, recording and coding what we observed. We also measured the progress of the learners from these classes. To do this we used:

- an assessment that required three pieces of free writing in response to a simulated magazine. This was marked using a mark scheme that took into account functional adequacy and word-, sentence- and text-level skills;
- a simple questionnaire on learners' confidence in writing at home, in the classroom and at work or in a public place; and
- a list of uses of writing. Learners were asked to tick those they had used in the past week.

In addition we interviewed 98 learners, spoke with teachers in each of the classes and collected examples of session plans, teaching materials and learners' work.

The findings

The findings that speak most directly to teachers came from a comparison of the nine classes that made the most progress in the writing assessment and the nine classes that made least progress. These findings are listed on the page opposite.

The key finding was that the classes that made the most progress were generally those where the focus of the teaching was on meaningful writing tasks rather than on exercises to practise discrete skills and in these classes learners spent time composing their own texts.

"...the classes that made the most progress were generally those where the focus... was on meaningful writing tasks... and learners spent time writing their own texts."

This book

In this book we build on these findings and explore ways in which teachers can make writing as communication the starting point for their teaching and encourage and support learners to write. In doing this we draw on other findings from the research study as well as on wider research, some of which was reviewed in the initial literature review. We also draw on the expertise and experience of practitioners to interpret the findings in relation to their everyday experience in the classroom and to share examples of practice.

Research findings

Features of the classes that made *most* progress

Compared to the classes that made least progress, learners spent:

- more time on contextualised writing tasks;
- more time on writing tasks at text level; and
- less time on word-level activities.

The researchers who observed the classes noted that:

- learners spent time composing meaningful texts;
- teachers set up tasks carefully before learners were asked to write;
- time was given to discussion of writing tasks in the full group;
- exercises designed to introduce and practise spelling, grammar and punctuation were discussed in the full group and were often explicitly linked to a task involving extended writing; and
- individual feedback and support, which took account of learners' individual needs, was provided while learners were engaged in the process of writing.

Features of the classes that made *least* progress

In a number of the classes that made the least progress the researchers observed:

- a lot of de-contextualised writing activity;
- a lot of time spent on activities at word and sentence level;
- individual learners' needs were met through individual tasks and worksheets; and
- limited time was given to the setting up of writing tasks.

Different aspects of writing and different starting points

Writers and researchers have distinguished between different types of writing skills. Practitioners in England will be familiar with the distinctions between text-, sentence- and word-level skills as used in the Adult Literacy Core Curriculum (Basic Skills Agency, 2001). Tricia Hedge (1992) makes a different but useful distinction between 'authoring' or 'creative skills' and 'crafting' or 'secretarial skills'. In this book we refer to the latter as 'technical skills'.

Authoring or creative skills:

- Thinking about the purpose for writing
- Thinking about the needs of the reader
- Deciding what to say
- Deciding how to say it

Technical, crafting or secretarial skills:

- Grammar
- Spelling
- Punctuation
- Handwriting

Learners have to develop both sets of skills if they are to develop as writers. The question is: how?

Text comes first

In the review of practice we found that many learners believed that they needed to master the technical aspects of writing before they tried to use writing to express their own ideas. In the research study our observations suggested that a number of teachers were reinforcing this belief. Diagnostic assessment, individual smart targets and the need to prepare learners for national qualifications encouraged some teachers to focus almost exclusively on the technical skills of writing. However, the findings of the project suggest that learners make best progress when the starting point is writing as communication and learners have the opportunity to experience the role of author. Getting the technical aspects right then becomes part of the process of saying something meaningful in writing rather than the main focus.

This approach is supported by the quotations below. The first comes from a set of materials for teachers developed as part of the 'Write where you are' campaign run by NIACE in 2006. We include several references to these materials throughout this book. The second is from an article written by Philip Pullman, author of *His Dark Materials* and other children's novels, in which he is commenting on the National Curriculum for schools. The third is taken from the Core Curriculum for Adult Literacy.

> *Teaching writing with adult students is best done by starting with the text and leaving worries about sentence and word structures till later. To put it another way; the most useful thing we can do is to help students to first focus on the meaning they want to create, not on providing them with lists of spelling patterns or grammar rules. Spelling work can grow out of the words they have decided they want. Grammar and punctuation is best done once there is some draft text to do it on.* (Mace, J. and Tomlinson, K. 'Write where you are' teacher materials, **http://www.niace.org.uk**)

> *So what I say is: back to basics.... They're often held to be things like spelling and grammar.... But the joy of discovery, the thrill we feel when an idea strikes that might become a story. If that joy isn't nourishing the roots of the work, it's never going to show in the flower. That truly is basic. I'm all for the basics.* (Pullman, 2002)

> *The writing tasks that learners are asked to undertake need to be varied and meaningful, however basic, with an emphasis on communication. Learners need to practise writing at text level even when their grip on individual words is shaky. Otherwise the understanding of the structures of written language, which they have gained through reading, won't be transferred to their own writing.* (Adult Literacy Core Curriculum, Basic Skills Agency, 2001)

Theories of writing

There is not space in a publication of this size to do justice to the theories of writing and writing development that have informed both research and practice but some suggested reading on this is provided at the end of the section. However, it is perhaps important to point out that current practice, as described in this guide, draws on a range of different approaches to writing and to learning more generally. In Section 4 we focus on writing as a process, a view of writing informed by cognitive psychology. We also introduce the concept of 'genre' which arose from the work of linguists, notably M.A.K. Halliday, who were concerned with the relationships between the grammatical form of language and its communicative function. In Sections 2 and 7 we describe practice that reflects a humanistic view of adult learning. The starting point for Section 5 is a social practice view of literacy.

Writing as social practice

Academics and practitioners who support the view of literacy as social practice argue that writing is not simply a set of skills. They talk of writing practices that are situated in the specific contexts of people's lives.

> We always read and write something, for a particular purpose, in a particular way, in a particular time and place. (Ivanič et al., 2006)

This perspective on writing challenges us to consider how the writing we teach in the classroom relates to the ways in which learners use writing in their everyday lives, the contexts for these writing practices and the social relationships they represent. It encourages us think about how we as teachers value and build on these uses of writing.

Reflect

Look at the research findings and the quotations above. Thinking about your own teaching context, what questions do these raise for you?

- If your questions relate to the research study, it may help to read the report of the research.
- If they relate to your teaching or to your learners, note these down and return to them after reading the rest of the book.

If you want to find out more

Grief, S., Appleby, Y., Hodge, R., Tusting, K. and Barton, D. (2007) *Effective Teaching and Learning: Writing*. London: NRDC.

Mace, J. and Tomlinson, K. (2006) 'Write where you are' teacher materials, **http://www.niace.org.uk**

For more on theory and research on writing

Hyland, K. (2002) *Teaching and Researching Writing*. Pearson Education.

Ivanič, R., Meyer, B. and Burgess, A. (2006) *Linking Learning and Everyday Life: A Social Perspective on Adult Language, Literacy and Numeracy Classes*. London: NRDC.

Kelly, S., Soundranayagam, L. and Grief, S. (2004) *Teaching and Learning Writing: A Review of Research and Practice*. London: NRDC.

3 Introducing learners to writing

How can we enable learners to experience success in writing and feel the 'joy of discovery, the thrill when an idea strikes' that Philip Pullman speaks of, especially when their technical skills are weak? This section explores this question. It includes a range of strategies teachers use to reduce learners' anxieties or their reluctance to write and provides a range of examples of activities that practitioners have used successfully with classes of different kinds.

Create a supportive atmosphere

First and foremost we need to create an atmosphere of trust in the classroom. Jane Mace, in the quotation below, highlights the sense of vulnerability we all experience as writers.

> It has always seemed to me that writing is a risky business. Every time we allow someone else to read a fragment of our writing, we reveal something of ourselves to them. Our fear is that what we reveal will be our weakness, not our strength: a poverty of expression, a weakness in spelling or grammar. Sometimes, however, there can be surprise. When we come to read back our own writing, not all of it is rubbish. Somewhere in the middle of it all will be a gem that, until then, we had not known was there: a new thought, a recalled memory. (Mace, 2005)

Storytelling

Kath Swinney

Storytelling can enable writing. If the teacher is truly interested in each learner's story and explicitly teaches listening skills, an atmosphere of trust and empowerment can develop in a group. Each story is given validity when it has been genuinely listened to. This is often the motivation needed to record that story in writing. Once trust has been established the technical issues such as spelling and grammar can be shared.

An example of a story developed in this way is included in Section 6, p. 53–54.

Reduce the load

Learners we interviewed for the initial review of practice highlighted the challenges writing can present:

It's harder 'cos you have to have the ideas in your head first.

You have to think of your own words and know how to write them.

Writing is much more difficult, there's a lot more involved.

For new writers writing places a heavy load on the working memory. It requires:

- the physical skill of handwriting or typing;
- the organisation of ideas;
- the choosing of words and the creation of sentences and paragraphs; and
- the detail of spelling and punctuation.

The examples included in this section illustrate ways in which teachers can reduce the load on beginner writers by providing support with one or more of these demands.

Reducing the load:

- Talk about the task
- Break the task down into stages
- Talk about the subject
- Collect and record ideas for vocabulary before writing
- Provide spellings
- Provide a model
- Provide a frame
- Write in groups
- Scribe for the learner

Talk can be work

Research finding

When learners were interviewed many of them told the researchers that they appreciated the opportunities for discussion about writing in their classes.

Overall the classes in which learners made most progress spent a high percentage of class time on talk. We observed teachers who spent considerable periods of time on discussion before learners started to write.

Discussion provides an opportunity to share experiences, stimulate memory, try out and rehearse ideas and opinions and tease out the right vocabulary. It can help to make links between the classroom task and learners' experience. It also gives teachers opportunity to listen to what learners already know about writing and to build from this.

Sometimes it is helpful for teachers and learners to have a frame for talk. This might be very similar to a writing frame or to the visual aids to planning discussed in Section 4. It can also be helpful for the teacher to model the talk, using her contributions as an example for learners to follow.

It doesn't have to be right first time

Learners often assume that good writers simply get it right first time. We know that all writers need to organise their thoughts before they write, that writers often change what they have written and that they then check it through carefully. Sharing this with learners can be reassuring. It can remove the pressure and free them to focus first on what they want to say and then return to work on the technical bits they find difficult. Teaching writing as a process is explored further in Section 4.

Provide a model

If you want a story you need to tell a story. You need to write yours. You get what you give. (Quote from a teacher)

It can be very helpful to have an example of the type of writing that is expected for a particular purpose. Even as experienced writers we often look for models when we attempt a new type of writing task.

Provide a frame

The Adult Literacy Core Curriculum (Basic Skills Agency, 2001) defines a writing frame as 'a structured prompt to support writing'.

A writing frame may provide:

- opening phrases for paragraphs;
- topics or questions for paragraphs;
- pictorial prompts for paragraphs;
- headings for sections of the text;
- linking phrases or connectives;
- a template for the particular text type; and
- suggested vocabulary.

Learners need more or less support depending on their experience in writing and the level of difficulty of the task. For example, a set of carefully structured questions can elicit sentence answers that together create a simple text. However, it is possible to use a very open frame with a mixed ability group. Learners write simple sentences or fuller paragraphs depending on their level. An example of a frame of this kind is included on p. 16. The *Skills for Life* learning materials include useful examples of writing frames.

Writing together

Working on a piece of writing with other people happens more commonly in everyday life than we tend to think. Asking learners to work together in small groups on a piece of writing can enable them to share their strengths and help to reduce the pressure on the individual writer. Section 7 focuses on collaborative writing.

ICT as a motivation to write

For some learners ICT can help to overcome a reluctance to write.

> Research highlights ICT as a great motivator in work with young adults. Learners
> find it attractive, engaging and something that signals the learning to be 'different
> from school.' (Skills for Life Quality Initiative, 2006)

Online games, blogs and wikis and the growing social uses of the web offer opportunities to engage young people in writing, and innovative work has been undertaken with mobile technology such as mobile phones and palmtops. Useful examples of how these can be used with Skills for Life learners, including those quite new to ICT, can be found in the parallel publication on research into practice in IT (Nance, Kambouri and Mellar, 2007).

PowerPoint can be used successfully with beginner writers, as the examples on p. 21 illustrate. The format of a slide naturally limits the length of text possible. Posters and invitations can also be made with relatively basic IT skills yet the finished products appear attractive and professional to the writer. This immediate success encourages learners to write more.

Scribing for the learner

Working with the teacher or a learning assistant who acts as a scribe can enable beginner writers to experience what it means to compose a piece of writing and see their own words written down or in print. Working together in this way is often referred to as the 'Language Experience' approach. As Jane Mace points out (Mace, 2004), this can be more than dictation; it can be a collaborative activity with the learner and teacher producing a text together. This approach can also help to develop speaking and listening and reading.

Delay assessment

The great majority of teachers we observed for the research study asked learners to do a piece of free writing as part of their diagnostic assessment. Careful analysis of this can provide a great deal of information for the teacher. It can also provide a valuable starting point for a conversation between the teacher and the learner about individual learning goals in writing. However, this can be daunting for some learners. It can help to delay the assessment until the learner has experienced success in some taster activities, of the type illustrated later in this section. This can help the learner to produce writing that does more justice to their skills and is more useful for the teacher.

Functional and expressive writing

Many of the activities used in this section focus on 'expressive' writing rather than the 'functional' writing more often associated with adult literacy. Adults have differing needs for functional writing such as forms, reports, invoices, letters and it is important that these are addressed through group and individual learning plans. Learning to deal with such tasks independently can be empowering.

> *I usually ask me mum... I thought 'no I'm going to do it myself'.* (Talking about a letter to the Passport Office)

> *I got to do a final draft then post it to school.* (A response to a Police Watch letter)

Expressive writing is also important. When we asked the learners we interviewed to share a piece of writing they were proud of, many chose to share pieces of expressive writing. Ursula Howard argues that there is a pressing case for including expressive writing within *Skills for Life* teaching. She suggests that, 'learning to write for self-expression builds a learner's sense that they have something to say' (Howard, 2006). Many of the examples provided in this section can do just that.

> *...it is not just functional writing that is important; for many adults personal writing is a key to understanding and sharing their experiences.* (Adult Literacy Core Curriculum, Basic Skills Agency, 2001)

Beginner writers are not beginner thinkers

It is essential to remember that the learners may be beginners at written English but they are not beginners in life. (Spiegel and Sunderland, 2006, p. 75)

Referring to the writing frame below, the teacher who created it wrote; 'Using the Martin Luther King speech and writing frame enables learners to broaden their vision and think about the future. It is a vehicle for aspirational and political thinking and writing. It starts with the personal and then embraces global ideas. The image of black and white children holding hands is as poignant today as in 1964 and enables learners to discuss serious issues such as racism'. The piece of writing by Zahra (p. 17) was written as a result of this activity.

A writing frame

The following frame was used together with an extract of Martin Luther King's famous speech and a photo of Martin Luther King speaking.

I Have a Dream...
I say to you today, my friends, I have a dream...

Write your dreams for <u>yourself</u>, family and friends here

Write your dreams for the <u>world</u> here

...I have a dream today!

Martin Luther King – I Have A Dream...

I say to you today, my friends. And so even though we face the difficulties of today and tomorrow, I still have a dream. It is a dream deeply rooted in the American dream.

I have a dream that one day this nation will rise up and live out the true meaning of its creed: We hold these truths to be self-evident that all men are created equal.

I have a dream that one day on the red hills of Georgia the sons of former slaves and the sons of former slave owners will be able to sit down together at the table of brotherhood.

I have a dream that one day even the state of Mississippi, a state sweltering with the heat of injustice, sweltering with the heat of oppression, will be transformed into an oasis of freedom and justice.

I have a dream that my four little children will one day live in a nation where they will not be judged by the color of their skin but by the content of their character. I have a dream today!

I have a dream that one day, down in Alabama, with its vicious racists, with its governor having his lips dripping with the words of interposition and nullification; one day right down in Alabama little black boys and black girls will be able to join hands with little white boys and white girls as sisters and brothers. I have a dream today!

I Have a Dream...

I have a dream that one day the people of Somalia will stop the war. I have a dream that one day this nation will rise up and join hands and rebuild their destroyed country and bury their differences.

I have a dream that one day the nation of Somalia will be transformed into an oasis of freedom and justice. I have a dream that one day the nation of Somalia will live by the true meaning of their beliefs.

I have a dream that one day the people of Somalia will create equal rights for men and women.   **By Zahra**

The following examples illustrate activities teachers have used to help learners experience writing.

Magnetic words

Kate Roberts

This activity was used with young people who had just left care. They had limited concentration and little interest in 'learning'.

I put up a magnetic board in the coffee bar/chill-out area at the beginning of a session with a sentence or phrase posted on it. I left other words on the board or in the box beside it. I didn't spell out or introduce the activity to them as a group but people were curious as I was setting it up and asked questions. I told them that they could add a word or sentence or their own thoughts if they wanted to. Most of the group made a contribution over the session as they passed through the area, anything from a phrase to a paragraph. Some of the end products were very creative and there was always the challenge of trying to create things that sounded rude!

The following session I took along what had been created written up on a large piece of paper. This often led to interesting discussions – Who had changed their bit? Was that really the best word to use in that sentence? It led to some rewriting and the use of a thesaurus and dictionary to check meanings or find better alternatives. Most of the pieces were on areas of interest such as 'LUV' or relationships, drugs, music etc. The learners were involved in putting together a monthly magazine that went out to all the care and foster homes and regularly produced pieces created from the poetry board.

Why did it work?

- The learners could choose to contribute or not. There was no pressure to do so.
- They could steer the writing towards a subject of their choice.
- It did not require them to spend ages on the task. They could add bits throughout the session.
- The words were provided for them so they were not hung up on spelling.
- It allowed them to collaborate, each doing what they were comfortable with. For example people would help search for the words others wanted to use.

- It allowed them to change things easily, move words and phrases around or change or add a word.
- It allowed them to be creative without being faced with a blank sheet of paper and having to think what to write.

Oral presentations

This activity was used with a GCSE group.

I asked the learners to prepare a presentation for the group on a topic in which they were interested and to design any visual aids etc. they wanted to use.

On the face of it this was a speaking task, but it quickly involved writing in the form of making notes and planning PowerPoint slides. In this way learners were drawn into writing without anxiety.

Why did it work?

- The learners did not perceive it as a writing task.
- The learners were writing about a topic in which they were interested and had knowledge or expertise.

The writing had a clear purpose, related to the presentation.

Haiku

Kate Roberts

This activity has been tried and tested with a wide range of literacy and ESOL learners in both community and college classes.

Many learners want to write creatively but are put off by the thought that to do so they need to write at length. A Haiku is not only short but it provides a clear structure for people to follow.

Haiku – A Japanese verse form in three lines and 17 syllables (5/7/5). It usually has two connected thoughts or ideas that conjure up a picture for the reader.

Leaves/ of/ bronze/ and/ gold	(5)
Cas/ca/ding /slow/ly /down/wards	(7)
nights /start /draw/ing /in	(5)

CASE STUDY

CASE STUDY

- I read and discuss examples of Haiku poems with the learners and examine the framework.
- With the group, I identify a theme for the Haiku and everyone is encouraged to suggest words and phrases that could be used. I write these up for sharing and for use in the syllabification activity.
- I use an activity on syllabification to check understanding and ability to break words up accurately into syllables. (I usually do this as a group activity using the words and phrases the learners have contributed on an agreed theme or topic. It ensures that those who aren't confident with this process have a range of words and phrases with the syllables already identified.)
- I encourage learners to write in pairs or small groups, to build confidence and encourage sharing of expertise and experience.
- At the end of a session I encourage those who wish to share what they have produced to do so. (Usually very positive feedback and encouragement is given by other students.)

The pieces are finally word processed with added borders or pictures that relate to the theme.

Why did it work?

- It provides a framework.
- The task isn't daunting (short and achievable).
- People feel comfortable and supported working as part of a group or in pairs.
- I provide words and phrases so reducing anxiety about spelling.
- It is fun and boosts confidence.
- There is an end product!
- It values creative forms from other cultures. ESOL learners can share and compare and contrast creative forms from their own culture. (A group of Japanese visitors to the centre were astonished and delighted to see a display of Haiku on the wall and it provided a real talking point between them and the students.)

Examples of Haiku created by learners

On the theme of autumn:

Sharp against the sky
the barren limbs of winter
glow in amber light

Yellow, red, gold, brown
lie drifts of fallen splendour
dying on the ground

On the theme of sherbert lemons:

Lemon shaped bon-bons
anticipate the moment
sherbert floods the mouth

Sweet, sour and tangy
tastebuds tingle, tantalized
citrus explosion

Writing with Pre-entry Learners

Alison Bagshaw

My group of learners had a range of additional needs and included some who had been assessed as working at Milestones 6, 7 and 8. All were keen to learn how to use the computer, so we decided to use PowerPoint in developing their writing. We decided to use these headings: 'My favourite things', 'What makes me happy', 'What makes me sad', and 'What I want to do in the future'. They were shown how to select a slide design and had fun choosing which to use. They all learned how to insert text and wrote sentences collaboratively using the headings to help them. We used a writing frame to suggest ideas for their favourite things. Some learned to insert a picture or photo as an illustration, while others downloaded pictures from clipart. The learners were all very proud of their finished work and grew in confidence. They have since presented their slide show to an external audience. This is one learner's work.

My favourite things
- My favourite colour is red
- My favourite t.v programme Eastenders
- my favourite character is Alfie Moon
- My favourite song is Angels by Robbie Williams

- My name is Gareth Cadet
- In my family there is Gareth
- My Dad is called Dave
- My Mum is called Catherine

Things that make me happy
- Being able to do things by myself
- Drawing and painting
- Drinking shandy

What I want to do in the future
- I want to be a comedian
- I want to be in Eastenders
- I want to be an artist

More ideas to encourage learners to write

Rap poems or songs

Dis Poetry (from 'City Psalms' by Benjamin Zephaniah)

Dis poetry is like a riddim dat drops
De tongue fires a riddim dat shoots like shots
Dis poetry is designed fe rantin
Dance hall style, big mouth chanting,
Dis poetry nar put yu to sleep
Preaching follow me
Like yu is blind sheep,
Dis poetry is not Party Political
Not designed fe dose who are critical

(http://www.benjaminzephaniah.com)

The learners (16–19 years old) were able to recreate their own songs in the same style and had great fun performing them like a rap.

Consequences

- Use the written form of the party game.
- Ask learners to read out the resulting stories.
- These can be used as the basis for a longer piece of writing.

Graffiti Walls

Writers write, right

Speech bubbles for cartoons

This can be fun to do on computer. It can also be helpful as a prompt for discussion about the differences between speech and writing.

Using photographs, for example of a shared trip

Learners can:

- write captions or sentences to go with the photos of their choice (using words and phrases from the board)

or

- place the photos in a sequence to tell a story (this can be done orally first) then write a sentence or more for each picture. (You can introduce connectives and conjunctions to link these.)

Those with good ICT skills and working at Level 1/2 can create a storyboard adding speech bubbles and comments to go alongside the narrative.

Starter sentences

- Select a topic and provide opportunity to discuss this as a whole group or in small groups.
- Provide the beginnings of sentences for learners to complete.
- Share and discuss the completed sentences and use these to create a shared text.

Drama bag

Put a collection of items in a bag. Ask each learner to take one out and describe it. Discuss what this tells you about the person who owned the bag. Use this as a starting point for a story or play.

Reflect

Teachers of adults are very aware that learners in literacy classes are not 'beginners in life'. Which of the strategies or activities discussed in this chapter could help the learners you work with to write something that they feel reflects their experience, knowledge, skills or interests?

If you want to find out more

Examples of learners' writing and guidance on teaching writing

Spiegel, M. and Sunderland, H. (2006) *Teaching Basic Literacy to ESOL Learners*. LLU+, London South Bank University.

Haiku

The Poetry Society, Pictorial Charts Educational Trust Wall charts (1995).

Haiku Chart. Also numerous websites – Google 'Haiku'.

Scribing

Mace, J. (2004) 'Language Experience: What's going on?', *Literacy Today*, 39. (See articles on Literacy Trust website, **http://www.literacytrust.org.uk**)

'A note on scribing', 'Write where you are teacher materials'. At: **http://www.niace.org.uk**

Writing frames

DFES *Skills for Life* learning materials. These can be obtained free from Prolog. Telephone the DfES Publications Team on 0845 60 222 60 or email dfes@prolog.uk.com

'Share a day', Write where you are teacher materials. At: **http://www.niace.org.uk**

Using new technologies with literacy and ESOL learners

The parallel publication to this one focusing on the use of ICT (Nance, Kambouri and Mellar, 2007) includes many ideas for using ICT with *Skills for Life* learners applicable to the teaching of writing.

4 Writing is a process

Learners can hold assumptions about writing that hold them back as writers; for example that writing can be right or wrong or that their writing should be perfect the first time. In the review of literature we quote a number of writers who argue the need to focus not just on the writing that learners produce but on how they get there. They stress the importance of teaching learners to understand writing as a process if they are to become independent as writers.

This understanding, that even for good writers, creating a piece of writing is not straightforward but involves time for planning and checking and a messy process of revision, can be empowering for learners who often feel that their struggle with writing is an individual failure. It is important to find time to discuss this.

At its simplest the process of writing can be represented as three stages. This was summarised by one practitioner as:

PREWRITE   >>>>   **WRITE**   >>>>   **REWRITE**

We have used three stages to organise the content of this section. These look at:

■ activities for learners before they begin to write;

■ supporting learners as they write a first draft; and

■ helping learners to transform this into the final product.

A note of caution

It is important not to present a process that is too simple or too rigid. Many writers stress that writing involves interrelated and 'recursive' processes. For example, as we begin to organise words and sentences into a text we often see new connections or a different angle on a subject that makes us go back to our plan. In some cases, not all the possible stages of the process are applicable.

A: Before you write

We noted in Section 2 that teachers in the classes that made the most progress gave a lot of time to setting up writing tasks with the learners.

Stage 1: Think about the reader and the purpose of the writing

The teacher and the learner need to be clear about the readers and the purpose of any piece of writing. Together these will influence the type of text that is needed, or, in other words, the 'genre' (see p. 28). Encouraging learners to think about the readers and their needs is important at each stage of writing.

Stage 2: Collect your ideas or information

Collecting together ideas or information can involve:

- recalling memories or information;
- researching a topic;
- a stimulus activity such as reading, watching a film, a visit or a talk;
- a brainstorming session to spark ideas; and
- a debate to bring out the different sides of an argument.

At this stage it can be useful to make notes but mind maps can provide a powerful, visual way to develop and record ideas. See 'If you want to find out more', p. 36.

Stage 3: Organise your ideas or information

Visual methods can help to organise ideas and information. Diagrams and tables of different kinds can be used to record, group, classify or sequence information or to clarify relationships between items or strands in an argument. Geoff Petty describes a range of such 'graphic organisers' in his book *Evidence-Based Teaching* (Petty, 2006, chapter 10).

One group we observed drew around the outline of their hand and used the spaces in the thumb and the fingers to plan five paragraphs for a piece of writing about themselves.

Stage 4: Make a plan

Sometimes diagrams are sufficient as a plan. However we also observed learners:

- numbering items on their notes or diagrams;
- colour coding notes with highlighter pens;
- drawing arrows on notes to organise the content of paragraphs;
- making lists.

Modelling a plan

The teacher recorded learners' ideas on travelling to the class on foot or by bus on a spidergram. They discussed fact and opinion and identified all the facts. The teacher then introduced paragraphs and suggested that their first paragraph could be on advantages of going by bus. As learners identified points for this paragraph she wrote '+bus' next to them. For a second paragraph the advantages of walking were highlighted and '+walking' was written against these. The teacher suggested that the learners used a third paragraph to present their own opinions.

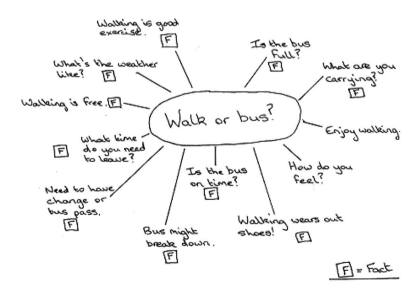

Genre

Genre refers to different forms of writing, for example a story, a report, a letter. Different genres have recognisable features of language and structure and it can help learners to become familiar with the features of the genres they need to master. Learners need to be introduced to models of the particular genre and to be supported to deconstruct these to identify the distinctive features.

For example, most instructional texts will:

- state a goal to be achieved, for example to bake a cake;
- state the materials needed, for example two eggs, and so on;
- use bulleted or numbered phrases that sequence the steps to take;
- include diagrams or illustrations;
- use imperative verbs in the present tense; and
- use signposting words for chronological order, for example first, next, finally.

> <u>Mix</u> the flour and salt in a bowl
>
> <u>Rub</u> in the butter
>
> <u>Beat</u> the egg
>
> <u>Add</u> the egg to the flour

Examples of activities

We observed several classes working on formal letters. The following are two examples of activities which were used to help learners to become familiar with features of this particular genre.

One group used a model letter that had been cut into sections and laminated. Practice in arranging these sections, for example the sender's address, the salutation, the main body of the text, helped them to become familiar with the conventions for the layout of a formal letter.

A teacher in another group identified three parts of the text that can be found in the main body of a formal letter. She explained these as the introduction to the subject, the main point or saying what you want, and the closing section. The learners then attempted to allocate sentences to a particular paragraph and to recreate a letter. After this they were given a sheet illustrating the structure as an 'aide memoire' and were asked to plan and write a formal letter of their own.

Teachers need to take care that they do not present genres in too rigid a way. Learners need opportunity to think critically about why genres exist and how they are used and by whom. As they develop as writers they need to feel free to adjust them to their own purposes, to question them or even to choose deliberately to ignore them.

B: The first draft

Stage 5: Write a first draft

At this stage we observed many teachers reminding learners to concentrate on what they wanted to say and not to worry about spelling and punctuation. The learners did not always find this easy.

> So absolute is the importance of error in the minds of many writers that 'good writing' to them means 'correct writing', nothing more. (Shaughnessy, 1977)

One key to encouraging learners to leave their dictionary to one side while they draft may be found in the way in which we respond to their writing. Our initial response sends a message to the learners about what we value most. The teacher is almost always the first, and sometimes the only person who will read what they have written. In our observations we noted many teachers praised learners' work but immediately moved into discussion of technical problems such as spelling or punctuation. If we want learners to focus initially on the communicative aspect of writing we need to model this for them and respond first and foremost as a reader to what they have to say, not as an assessor.

"...we need to ...respond first and foremost as a reader to what they have to say, not as an assessor."

Research finding

Each class was scored for a set of general teaching strategies based on those devised for a large study of ESOL literacy in the US (Condelli *et al*, 2003). One of these was:

> **The teacher is flexible and responds to the learners' concerns as they arise. Goes with the teachable moment.**

We found a positive link between teaching that was scored high on this strategy and learners' progress in the writing assessment.

Learners, and particularly those least confident in writing, often need support as they write. The research showed that teachers in the most successful classes spent a lot of time with individual learners at this stage, scaffolding the process and discussing queries. We observed many teachers taking advantage of 'the teachable moment' and providing mini-lessons in response to learners' questions.

C: Improving the first draft

Stage 6: Revise and redraft

Revision relates to what we have to say and the way in which we say it. Revision can be quite radical and can involve the reordering or rewriting of whole sections of text.

Before they attend to the details of spellings, punctuation, grammar and layout we need to encourage learners to think again about their purpose and their readers and to check whether they have put their message across clearly and effectively. They need to feel free to cut sections out and add bits in, to change the order of the text. It helps to model this process with them.

The *Cambridge Advanced Learner's Dictionary* defines the word 'edit' as 'To prepare a text or film for printing or viewing by correcting mistakes and deciding what will be removed and what will be kept in'. For learners it involves checking their writing prior to preparing a fair copy. Motivation for this stage in the process is likely to be greater when the writing task is authentic or the piece is to be made available to a wider readership (see Section 5).

Stage 7: Edit your work

Learners can find checking their own work difficult. The example on p. 34–35 illustrates how a teacher worked with a group of learners to model the processes of revision and editing using their own writing. This example also illustrates the value of word processing software for editing.

It may not be appropriate to correct every error. In some cases teachers and learners chose to focus on particular aspects of the writing, usually those they had discussed at the prewriting stage. It can also be important that both teachers and learners recognise that errors can be useful. They help teachers to assess what the learner knows and what still needs to be taught or practised. They also provide opportunity for the teacher to explain rules or patterns in context. Explicit discussion of this can be very helpful. (For more on errors and the technical aspects of writing see Section 6.)

Other suggestions for supporting revision and editing, drawn from the literature and from practitioners, include the following.

- Learners reading the work aloud, either to themselves or to others
- Learners using a set of criteria to check their piece of writing
- Asking learners to read and comment on each other's writing
- Going back to a model for the genre being used
- The teacher using the highlighter tool on electronic documents to scaffold revision and editing

In a useful publication on report writing in the workplace (Minton, 2004) learners are encouraged to check their draft reports using 'Five Cs'.

Check the report is:

- Clear
- Concise
- Correct
- Complete
- Courteous

One teacher illustrated the order in which she encouraged learners to check their work as an inverted triangle.

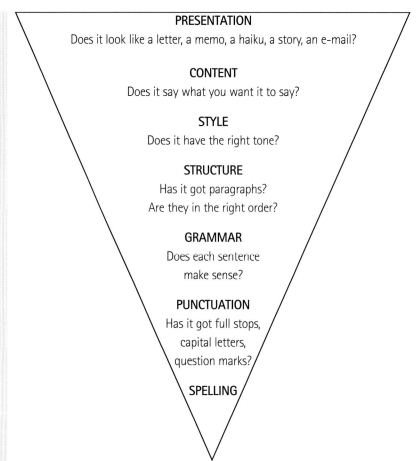

PRESENTATION
Does it look like a letter, a memo, a haiku, a story, an e-mail?

CONTENT
Does it say what you want it to say?

STYLE
Does it have the right tone?

STRUCTURE
Has it got paragraphs?
Are they in the right order?

GRAMMAR
Does each sentence
make sense?

PUNCTUATION
Has it got full stops,
capital letters,
question marks?

SPELLING

It is not easy to 'rewrite' as this is often a new concept for inexperienced writers. Tactics are needed to tackle a first draft. The idea of the triangle is that you start with the big picture and work down to the fine detail step by step. The triangle has a question at each step to enable the learner to address each issue. Spelling is dealt with last. Learners can underline spellings they are not sure about, check them with a spell check or a dictionary and then ask someone else to have a look. If you are teaching writing you can use the triangle as a scheme of work. Address an issue week by week in the skills part of your session while working on creative projects in the free writing part of your session.

Kath Swinney

Writing takes time

Some of the classes that made the most progress spent a long time on one piece of writing. This sometimes extended over several classes. In other cases learners continued with work at home. Time was allowed for the different stages of the writing process and there were plenty of opportunities for talk. In a number of cases the researchers commented on the way learners remained focused on a task once their interest was engaged.

The following example illustrates how a teacher explored her learners' thoughts on writing and the strategies they used when they wrote. It also offers a way to introduce the concept of writing as a process and to build this into classroom writing tasks.

Writing as a process

Jane Tones

Resources: Cards with one of the possible stages of the writing process written on each and a few blank. The idea for the cards comes from *Writing* (Hedge, 1992).

My initial aims were to encourage a class of young learners who 'hated writing':

- to deconstruct the writing process;
- to begin to view themselves as writers; and
- to eliminate some of their fear of writing by highlighting that writing is a process, not a specialised thing that some people can do and some people can't.

The activity

1. Invite learners to discuss writing and record their thoughts on a flipchart. Encourage learners to share their concerns:

- What do you find difficult about writing?
- How do you go about composing a piece of writing?
- How do you feel when you are asked to write something?

2. Explain the activity to the group and why we are going to do this. Go through the set of cards and discuss what each stage means. Ask learners to arrange the cards in the order that they approach writing. (Stress that there is no right or wrong way and that not all stages may be used by all people or for all types of writing.)

3.   Learners look at each other's stages and compare and discuss:

- similarities and differences;

- why it is helpful to know the different stages; and

- which stages people find the most difficult/the easiest.

4.   Elicit learners' ideas for each stage.

5.   Encourage learners to use these stages in a chosen piece of writing. Keep the cards out throughout a writing session and check with learners which stage they are working on as they undertake writing activities.

At the end of the writing session, return to the original flipchart and ask if any of the learners' concerns have been alleviated. Ask for feedback on the stages of the process they used and which aspects of this they feel they need to work on. Have their feelings towards writing changed at all?

Why did it work?

Learners are able to:

- break down a complicated process and tackle it in more manageable chunks;

- share their ideas and concerns;

- see the importance of discussion and generating ideas amongst themselves before beginning to write and see that this is a legitimate part of the process; and

- identify their own strengths in writing and areas to improve on.

Using a digital display board to revise writing as a group

Taken from an observation of a course on writing and computers.

The class was working on an email letter. They had to imagine that they were the manager of a restaurant who had received a letter of complaint from a customer, and they now had to write a reply. The class had written a first draft of this letter in the previous lesson.

The teacher had taken all the learners' first drafts and had removed their names. One of the problems in the learners' first drafts was that they had omitted a lot of essential words, so where this had happened she had inserted a dash, to indicate a missing word.

The teacher gathered the learners around the central table and asked them to look at the digital display board, while she sat at the computer nearest the board. She put one email letter at a time onto the digital display board and took the learners through it a sentence at a time asking them to suggest improvements. All the learners were very involved with the task, and there was plenty of lively discussion. The teacher's skilled questioning kept the learners' focus on the audience and purpose of the email. She asked questions such as 'what would you think if you read this letter?', 'what does the manager want the customer to think when she gets this letter?', 'how can we make this clearer?' As the learners made suggestions for improvements, the teacher typed them in so the learners could see the revised sentence immediately. It helped them to see that as writers they could make choices about how to express themselves and to consider the effects of their writing on their readers.

These learners tended not to read their own writing with sufficient care. This exercise forced them to re-read carefully and to note the fine detail of the writing, such as whether they had chosen the best word for their intended purpose, whether any words were missing, or whether the spelling was correct. They did not have to worry about writing or typing and were free to concentrate on the process of revision. The technology enabled them to see the impact of their proposed revisions immediately, and if they wanted to, they could revise it again to make further improvements.

Reflect

The research project suggests that it is important not to rush writing tasks and that talking about writing is important. Think about the way you plan for writing. How much time do you allow for learners to complete a piece of writing? How explicitly do you discuss writing as a process?

Seven stages have been used to illustrate the process of writing in this section. What would you put on the cards for the activity on p. 33? Try out the activity. Do the learners in your classes identify other stages?

If you want to find out more

Writing as a process

The review of literature undertaken for the first writing project includes a summary of the insights that viewing writing as a process has produced and the implications of this view on the teaching of writing. See Kelly *et al.*, (2004) (Section 2.3.1 on p. 13 and 2.62 p. 17).

'Process and stages activity': 'Write where you are teacher resources' **http://www.niace.org.uk**

The value of errors

Shaughnessy, M.P. (1977) *Errors and Expectations: A Guide for the Teacher of Basic Writing.* Oxford University Press.

Graphic organisers

Petty, G. (2006) *Evidence-Based Teaching.* Nelson Thornes.

Genre

http://www.standards.dfes.gov.uk – Search for 'Language across the curriculum', Training Pack. See section on 'Writing non-fiction'.

Spiegel, M. and Sunderland, H. (1999) *Writing Works: Using a Genre Approach for Teaching Writing to Adults and Young People in ESOL and Basic Education Classes.* LLU+, London South Bank University.

Writing for the workplace

Minton, C, (2004) *Report Writing at Work.* Suffolk County Council, Training Matters. This and other titles on writing in the workplace are available from Avanti Books: **http://www.avantibooks.com**

Mind maps

- Put 'mind maps' into Google
- Download 'Inspiration' software: **http://www.inspiration.com**
- Tony Buzan: see **http://www.buzanworld.com**
- For a case study on using mindmaps on computer for literacy learners and more websites see the parallel guide on ICT (Nance, Kambouri and Mellar, 2007).

5 Looking beyond the classroom

Most adult literacy learners do some writing outside the classroom. In this section we look at some of the evidence from the research project on learners' current uses of writing, their needs and aspirations and the degree to which teachers make links between these and the writing tasks in the classroom.

In Section 2 we made reference to the social practice approach to adult literacy and the implications of this for our understanding of the role writing plays in learners' lives. The following quotations reflect this approach.

> *Tutors should make listening to learners, and gaining knowledge of learners' lives, motivations, interests and capabilities, the cornerstone of their pedagogy.* (Ivanič *et al.*, 2006)

> *At a time when the field of adult language, literacy and numeracy is becoming more structured in England and elsewhere, with assessment, targets, a core curriculum and teacher training, it is important to reflect upon what the meaning and purpose of literacy and numeracy is in the lives of the people who come to learn.* (Appleby *et al.*, 2007)

We asked the learners we interviewed how they used writing outside the classroom and about their needs and aspirations in relation to writing. Their responses included a wide range of uses and contexts for writing and the spidergram on p. 39 provides a taste of these.

A suggested activity for an established group

- Working as a whole class or in smaller groups encourage learners to brainstorm all the times they (and possibly their families) have used writing in the last week.
- Ask learners to create a spidergram of the kind illustrated on p. 39.
- With the learners, agree on different ways in which these uses might be grouped
- Introduce the use of tables to classify different types of writing or different uses of writing

■   Encourage learners to explore distinctions such as formal and informal writing or personal, creative and transactional writing (writing to get things done)

An activity of this type could:

■   enable the teacher to gain a better picture of the writing learners already undertake;

■   extend the learners' understanding of writing and different types of writing;

■   generate discussion on, for example, the influence of technology on writing; and

■   provide a starting point for making links between writing inside and outside the classroom.

The research interviews also gave us insights into learners' attitudes to writing and the importance they attached to writing of different types. (See quotes on page 40.) Sharing perceptions and discussing experiences of writing outside the classroom can allow teachers and learners to stand back and take a critical look at the ways in which writing is used in society and how this relates to issues of status and power.

> *Critical literacy education looks out beyond the classroom, enabling learners to reflect on the relationship between literacy and their own material and social circumstances. In this way literacy can become 'a resource for people acting back against the forces that limit their lives.'* (Crowther, Hamilton and Tett, 2001, taken from Grief *et al.*, 2007, p. 45)

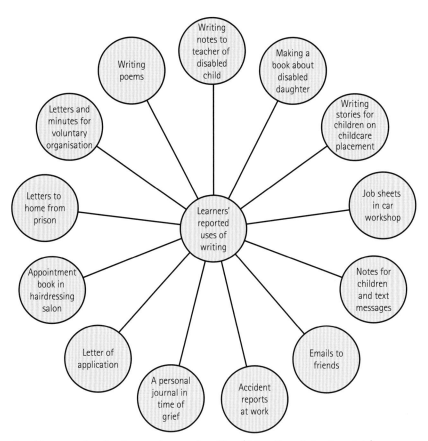

A spidergram showing learners' uses of writing (Taken from interview data)

These examples could be grouped in different ways

Writing for:	Examples
Children	
Work	Job sheets
?	
?	*Ask learners to help you decide on other groupings*
?	

Type of writing:	Examples
Personal	*Journals and diaries*
Transactional	*Appointment book entries*
Creative	

Building on the writing learners already do

The learners interviewed for the research project tended to undervalue the writing they already did outside class. Some referred to the writing they were learning to do in class as 'proper' writing.

...only quick writing, informal, to get the meaning across, short sentences. I don't need to write at work.

I only write in class. Oh, I do text messages on my mobile phone. I write notes to my daughter in the house.

...notes at home, texting, booking appointments in the salon.

...messages for work and for my children, time sheets and accident report at work.

He feels that the extended writing he has done... is not the kind of writing he will do when he gets back to work. This kind of writing is more functional, e.g. writing invoices, taking notes from phone messages.

Reflect

Are there ways in which you can build on the writing with which learners already feel confident, to make a bridge to what they feel is 'proper writing'? Here are three ideas based on the learners' comments above.

- Make use of mobile phones in class. Ask learners to contribute ideas via text messages.

- Ask a learner to teach another learner how to complete her timesheet or how to write an invoice.

- Translate a text message into a handwritten phone message and then into a formal letter. Swap letters and reverse the process.

Research finding

Where teachers did make links between the teaching in the classroom and learners' lives outside the classroom the analysis indicated that learners were more likely to report increased confidence in writing at home.

Taking account of learners' needs and interests

It is no surprise that learners feel more confident in writing tasks at home when teachers relate the teaching of literacy to life outside the classroom. However, we found that teachers made such links in only a small proportion of the teaching sessions we observed. Although session plans and individual learning plans often took careful account of learners' needs in relation to the core curriculum for literacy, they more rarely took account of the contexts in which learners needed to write outside the classroom.

Where learners spoke of their interests and aspirations, the links between these and their work in class were often very tenuous. Few were working on writing tasks that they would need in their current or future roles.

Comments in inspection reports indicate that inspectors place importance on real life contexts for writing:

> *...some activities are not linked sufficiently to a real life context. Skills learned are not always applied. For instance, a student whose individual learning plan targeted improvements in free writing continued to practise punctuation through worksheets.*

> *The goals often relate just to accreditation and are not set in a relevant context.*

Shared contexts for writing

In some teaching situations learners share a real life context, for example learners on the same vocational course, parents attending a family literacy course or employees on a workplace course. In the research study we observed:

- army recruits working on writing projects relating to their regiment;
- a group of NVQ hairdressing students evaluating and reporting on hair products.

In both cases the learners commented positively on the links made with their chosen work. Research by the NRDC indicates a strong link between embedded teaching of language, literacy and numeracy and learners' retention and achievement in these subjects for learners on vocational courses.

Learners' lives do not always offer opportunity to use the writing skills they develop in class (see quotes on p. 40). Some learners told us in interview that they wanted to improve their writing for the sense of personal achievement or the intellectual challenge rather than to write for a particular purpose. Researching literacy practices and using writing tasks that have real purposes and audiences can however have real value in developing their understanding of writing.

Reflect

How much do you know about the purposes for which the learners you teach use writing outside the classroom or their needs and aspirations in terms of writing?

How do the learners you teach perceive the relationship between writing inside and outside the class? What are the implications of their perceptions for your teaching?

Look at the activity outlined on p. 39. Is this something you might do with learners in the courses you teach? If you try it, record what you learn and reflect on what changes you might make to your teaching as a result.

Authentic writing activities

A NIACE and NRDC publication for practitioners, *Responding to People's Lives* (Appleby and Barton, 2007) addresses how the idea of literacy as social practice can be translated into classroom practice. In this the authors argue that 'using authentic materials in authentic tasks for real purposes, helps to make links between learning and literacy... in people's everyday lives'.

In the research study on writing we attempted to test the effect of authenticity on learner's progress and confidence. The findings from the statistical analysis relating to the effects of authenticity were surprising and somewhat contradictory and readers who are interested are invited to refer to the research report for more detail. We did, however, note that authenticity was a strong feature in only a small proportion of classes. Although we observed authentic materials used for reading and exploration of genre, and several teachers responded to specific requests from individual learners for support with tasks such as letters and forms, we observed very few authentic writing tasks.

Providing opportunities to write for real audiences and real purposes in the classroom can be challenging. The following are examples drawn from the practitioners who worked on this publication.

Exploiting the potential of ICT

- Email exchanges with other class members or pen pals in other classes
- Blogs on a website or intranet
- Use of social networking websites such as MySpace, and wikis on the web
- Submitting writing for publication on the web through sites such as 'Skillswise – Your Stories'
- Creation of books for sharing with others
- Creation of posters or invitations for real events

Writing for children

- Stories for children (see p. 48)
- Writing up memories for children or grandchildren

Work-related activities

- Updating CVs
- Working on accident reports and other proformas and asking learners to bring in real examples from their workplace

Creating a real dialogue

- One practitioner asked learners to complete a learning diary which was part of their Individual Learning Plan. The following extract illustrates how this generated an authentic dialogue between learner and teacher.

Date	What have you learned today and how did you feel about it?	Reminders/ Comments
Week 4	I have work with Bruce today we have been doing our homework form last week I have really enjoyed working we bruce he help me with spelling we talk about ideas on what to do. Cant wait for next week	
Tutor Comments	*You did work well with Bruce and shared your ideas, which is what I wanted you to do. You produced a good, clear set of instructions, so well done for that. I was pleased to learn that you are enjoying working collaboratively with other people in the group and that you are getting a lot out of sharing ideas. Just remember that when you write someone's name it begins with a capital letter.*	
Week 5	I have worked with Bruce today we have been doing a list for visiting friends I have found it better this week because I felt more confident I have done a bit of spell grammar. I have gotten to like English now before I did not. hope you have a nice Christmas. I will see you next year cant wait	It's a spell and grammar checker that you have used.
Alison Bagshaw		

It can be difficult to define what we mean by 'authentic' in relation to learners' writing. One practitioner suggested that we can view a piece of writing as 'authentic' when, in writing it, 'we are truly being ourselves'. There are sometimes things that learners want to write about, that have particular relevance to their lives. If we create the right environment, listen to learners, and give them space to choose their own topics we can provide opportunity for such pieces of writing to happen.

Publishing learners' work

One way to provide a purpose and audience for learners' writing is to share it with a wider readership. Mace and Tomlinson in the 'Write where you are' materials provide a useful list of suggestions for publishing learners' writing ranging from posting a piece on a notice board to publishing it in a book or magazine. The Effective Practice Study on ICT found that the production of a finished artefact supported learners' motivation and the parallel publication to this one, which focuses on ICT (Nance, Kambouri and Mellar, 2007), provides examples, including ideas for a web space shared by a group of learners.

The publication of learners' writing is currently undergoing a revival and learners can be encouraged to write by introducing them to websites and books that include learners' work. See the section 'If you want to read more' below.

If you want to read more

Finding out about learners' contexts for literacy outside the classroom

Fowler, E. and Mace, J. (2005) *Outside the Classroom: Researching Literacy with Adult Learners.* Leicester: NIACE.

Social practice approach to literacy

Ivanič R., Appleby, Y., Hodge, R., Trusting, K. and Barton, D. (2006) *Linking Learning and Everyday Life: A Social Perspective on Adult Language, Literacy and Numeracy Classes.* London: NRDC.

Appleby, Y and Barton, D. (2007) *Responding to People's Lives.* Leicester: NIACE.

Publishing

'Write where you are', NIACE. At: **http://www.niace.org.uk** (Follow 'Starting points' then 'Edit and write'.)

Gatehouse books: **http://www.gatehousebooks.org.uk**

BBC RAW: **http://www.bbc.co.uk/raw/**

BBC Skillswise: **http://www.bbc.co.uk/skillswise/**

Voices on the Page: **http://www.nrdc.org.uk**

Nance, B., Kambouri, M. and Mellar, H. (2007) *Using ICT. Developing Adult Teaching and Learning: Practitioner Guides.* Leicester: NIACE.

6 | The technical aspects of writing

Research finding

When the learners we interviewed spoke about what they had learned or what they still needed to work on, more than three quarters referred to grammar, spelling, punctuation and handwriting.

This finding is not a surprise. These are the aspects of writing that learners are likely to remember as problems at school. They are also the very visual aspects of writing by which learners know their writing is still judged. Learners are right to place importance on spelling, grammar and punctuation as the following quote from the CBI confirms:

> A functionally literate employee should be expected to be able to observe the basic rules of grammar, be able to spell everyday words correctly, use capital letters and basic punctuation properly, and use a writing style appropriate to the situation. (CBI, 2006, p. 5)

The research study didn't look in detail at methods of teaching of spelling, grammar and punctuation. However, the assessment we used did measure how well learners were able to use what they had learned about these technical aspects of writing in their own texts. What helps learners to do this?

Research finding

When we looked at the classes that made most progress on the writing assessment and those that made least progress our findings seem to suggest that the following approaches can be helpful:

- ▪ Lots of opportunity to talk about aspects of spelling, grammar or punctuation.

- Making a clear link between the teaching of specific aspects of spelling, grammar or punctuation and a meaningful writing task.

- Supporting and providing explanations for individual learners while they are drafting, revising and proof-reading their own texts.

On the other hand, the findings suggest that the following approaches can be less helpful:

- Spending a lot of time on exercises that have no clear link to a meaningful writing task.

- Spending a lot of time on individual worksheets.

Since many adults bring with them powerful images of writing associated primarily with spelling, grammar, and handwriting, adult literacy educators should discover ways to help students learn to put this aspect of writing into perspective. Low-level writing processes such as spelling, handwriting, and grammar need to be taught not in isolation but along with the higher-level processes of learning so that these tools are applied to the construction of meaning. (Marilyn K. Gillespie, 1999)

The 'teachable moment'

Struggling to express ideas or share information in writing makes the learner engage with questions of choice of vocabulary, word order, spelling or punctuation in a very different way to that in which he or she engages with multiple choice questions based on a given text. In this context teachers' explanations are anchored in the communicative act of writing. The learner's desire to get something right can create the 'teachable moment'. In addition, as teachers provide support they have the opportunity to discover how much the learner understands and to assess how misunderstandings or gaps in knowledge can be addressed. This in turn can inform the teacher's plans for future sessions. Worksheets and computer based exercises can have a role where points have already been taught and revision or practice is needed.

CASE STUDY

Making a book for your child using the computer

Jan Chatterton

Parents attended a ten-week course where they spent part of each session creating a reading or number book for their child. The parents were taught how to create decorative borders and backgrounds, how to scan in photographs and use clipart to illustrate their texts, and how to use Wordart to make their headings lively and attractive. They regularly used Word, Publisher and the Internet.

The content of their individual books was discussed in detail with each parent to ensure it was appropriate for their children's age and stage of learning. This allowed the teachers to introduce the appropriate language and explain the ways reading and numeracy are taught nowadays and why. Parents explored modern methods and through this were motivated to improve their own skills as well.

With older children the family worked together to produce a family album to show other family members. This approach has been used successfully in many settings including libraries, youth clubs and community centres, as well as in schools.

- Parents were highly motivated because the books were for their children.
- They were determined their writing should be accurate and spent much time redrafting.
- Discussions around correct grammar, spelling and punctuation skills stemmed from individual questions and were rooted in the texts they were writing.
- Teachers produced supplementary information sheets to support accuracy and parents referred to them in class and took them home to use. They again related directly to the texts being written.
- Parents learned how to learn by hearing about and discussing modern teaching techniques within school. They became open to learning how to improve their own skills.

The learners we interviewed valued teachers who took time to explain the technical aspects of written English. They were delighted to be introduced to rules and patterns and to be given reasons or historical explanations for particular features of language.

The tutor speaking, explaining it, made it better. It put more depth. She showed me how to put words over.

She gives us the technical.

The teachers here will sit down and make time to explain.

Learning from learners' errors

In the review of literature we refer to the work of Mina Shaughnessy, whose book *Errors and Expectations* (1997) illustrates the value of learners' errors in understanding the problems they face as they attempt to write and in identifying strategies that might help them to overcome these.

The analysis on p. 50–51 illustrates what it is possible to learn from a piece of free writing. The writing came from a class observed for the research and was a first draft. It should be added that although in this case we look at just one piece, the teacher would have built up a knowledge of the learner's strengths and weaknesses over time, from an analysis of several pieces of writing.

The frame used for the analysis uses the same headings as those in the inverted triangle used with learners discussed on p. 32. The first column is intended to reflect what the teacher finds in the text, the second the teachers' immediate responses to the draft and the third, notes for future action.

Feedback to the learner

The following points are useful to bear in mind when responding to learners' work, either orally, by email, or by marking a paper version.

- Respond first as a reader rather than an assessor. Comment on what the learner has to say and the way in which he or she has said it (see p. 29).
- Always find something to praise before discussing what the learner can improve.
- Avoid overloading the learner. It can help to comment or mark selectively. This involves prioritising the learning points to share with the learner. Select points that:
    - link to previous learning;
    - the learner can generalise from and use in further tasks;
    - are relevant to the purpose of the particular task and the type of writing attempted. (For example if the learner were writing an accident report, it would be important to draw attention to the sequencing of the content and to highlight verbs that need to be in the past tense.)

- Check the learner's reasoning before launching into an explanation. For example; 'I noticed you wrote London in capitals and wondered why that was?'

- Ensure learners know in advance the criteria by which the writing will be judged.

- Where possible provide prompts for the learner to correct his or her own work.

The following example shows a teacher using this way of working:

In Camden its is all differents people from all differents cultures there are markets and shops restaurant Banks shoe shope and night clubs. In part of Camden there is a racist atmosphere. Most of it is young kids from different street. every week end me and my wife and my Daughter Go to the market and some time we Go to McDonald's for a meal.

Analysis	Response to learner	Notes for future sessions
Presentation: Continuous prose suitable for description.		
Content: It provides a flavour of the area and includes the features discussed. Good expansion of point about racist atmosphere.	Praise. Say that it gives you a flavour of the area. Ask open questions about the racism.	
Style: A good attempt at description of an area but has not described the markets, shops etc.	Ask questions to draw out more detail e.g. the sights, sounds, smells of markets, shops and restaurants.	
Structure: Moves from different cultures to racism and from general description to his own links to area. No attempt at paragraphs.	Once more detail has been added point out that the three sections could be made into separate paragraphs.	Discuss titles when needed for future writing task. Introduce/revise paragraphs.
Grammar: The sentence structure is good. Use of 'and' to make a compound sentence but no complex sentences. The writer's dialect may be causing the erratic use of 's' for plurals.	(Check whether learner uses complex sentences when learner has added detail.)	Discuss dialect and the differences between speech and writing. Provide models of complex sentences.

Analysis	Response to learner	Notes for future sessions
Punctuation: Some full stops used correctly. The writer knows that capital letters are needed for the start of sentences and for proper nouns but use erratic.	Encourage learner to proof read for full stops and commas.	
Spelling: Good. Using some given vocabulary.	Praise spelling.	

The following examples illustrate ways in which teachers who were observed for the research project linked teaching of the technical aspects of writing with meaningful writing activities.

Using the learners' own writing to teach grammar

A group created a poem together on the theme of the colour green. When this was completed the teacher used the poem to help the learners to identify the nouns they had used within the poem.

Using spellings arising from writing task

Teachers used the prewriting activities to elicit key words that learners might need in the writing task. In discussing these they both revised previously taught strategies and introduced new ones. It is important to offer a range of strategies and allow learners to choose those they find most useful.

In some classes learners had been taught how to use the 'Look, Say, Read, Cover, Write, Check' method for learning spellings and had been provided with booklets to use for this purpose. Learners were responsible for adding new words that they wanted to learn.

Addressing the specific demands of a particular writing task

The learners in one group had identified in their initial interviews that they would like to work on formal letters. At the start of the session the teacher and learners spent some time discussing subjects for formal letters that they might actually want to send. Having established the purposes and audiences

CASE STUDY

for their letters the group then looked at the structure of formal letters and the use of paragraphs before they went on to plan and draft their letters. The work on paragraphs was explicitly linked to the agreed task of writing a letter.

Alerting learners to a particular rule before writing

Learners were first asked to read a description of a shopping street. This piece was used in different ways:

- to encourage learners to think about a place where they go to shop or to eat,
- as a model for a description of a place,
- as a focus for an analysis of the use of capital letters for proper nouns.

After considerable discussion, learners drafted their own descriptions and in doing so were encouraged to take special care to use capitals for proper nouns where these were needed.

Using the 'teachable moment'

A learner had spent 35 minutes drafting a piece of descriptive writing. The teacher's initial response was praise. It focused on specific features of the writing where she recognised effort and improvement. She also picked out parts of the account she liked. She was a discerning and appreciative audience.

The teacher supported the process of checking, reminding the learner of previous learning about complete sentences, subject and verb. Her comments on the influence of his speech on his writing extended and developed that understanding.

The teacher read parts of the work aloud to the learner. This helped him to recognise some of the gaps and see where punctuation was needed. Her suggestions are tentative leaving the learner the responsibility to make changes. The copy of the draft provided later showed no corrections by the teacher on the script.

This example illustrates not only how a learner's skills in spelling and punctuation improved but how, supported by an atmosphere of trust, she was encouraged to share more of herself in writing.

Progress and how to expand a story

Story by Beatrice, comments by Kath Swinney

This story was told to our small class in a storytelling session and was later written up.

Wen I was boan my mother left me with my father one day she came for me I dint want to go so she went to the coat I went to live with my stepfather my mother left again my step father sister came to visit and she took me to live with her I worked in her house one day her sister came to visit she was pregnant she took me to the city to do her housework and look after her children one day we came to the UK I was at home looking after her children. Now I am happy because I can speak English and I come to school.

The sentence structure was perfect so I just had to explain that full stops can group the words together to make a unit of sense. Then I put in one simple question, 'How did you feel?' It was a story without the writer and I wanted her input. I also wanted to keep the question simple but open. The story developed.

This is a story about me. Wen I was born my mother left me with my father and I was very happy leving with my grandmother shes a nice lady. One day she came back to take me away from my grandmother well I dint want to go with my mother but she went to coat and she took my with her to live with my step dad sister well I dint like leving with my step dad sister she dint not care about going to school she only wanted me to look after her children...

The latest version came two months after the first one.

When I was born my mother left me with my grandmother I was very small and I didn't know what was going on but I was happy living with my grandmother I didn't go to school. I was small I didn't know what was good for me and one day my mother came back to take me with her but I didn't want to go with her and she went to the courthouse there was nothing I could do and I went with her. I was not happy because my mother didn't think that I needed to go to school. All she wanted was for me to work as a maid and give her the money....

CASE STUDY

The story is becoming more complex and we can begin to hear the writer's voice as a person who can express her thoughts and opinions. The story ends:

I was wondering what my life was going to be like without going to school. I could not speak English I was not very happy with my life. One day I dised [decided] to ask someone a bout how I can learn English. I was learning English and now I am very happy with my life the way it is now.

The punctuation and the spelling are developing as the writing develops. We have corrected her writing and I have pointed out relevant grammar or spelling points in other texts we have read but we have not done a single worksheet or exercise.

Her progress is extraordinary.

Reflect

Use the list of points on pp. 49–50 with a piece of writing done by one of the learners in your class then check your notes against the learner's Individual Learning Plan. Would it help to cross reference your notes to the core curriculum?

If you have opportunity for peer observation, agree to monitor each other providing feedback to learners on their work. You may find it helpful to use the points on pp. 49–50 as a checklist.

If you want to find out more

The training notes for teachers at Key Stage 3 produced by the Standards Unit have some useful suggestions. These can be ordered from Prolog or downloaded from the web. Go to **http://www.standards.dfes.gov.uk** and follow the links to Key Stage 3, English, Resources and publications.

Using learners' errors

Shaughnessy, M.P. (1977) *Errors and Expectations: A Guide for the Teacher of Basic Writing*. Oxford University Press.

Marking

See: **http://www.standards.dfes.gov.uk** – search for 'Language across the curriculum', Training Pack. See section on 'Marking for literacy'.

Spelling

Each unit of the DfES *Skills for Life* learning materials has a specific spelling section containing several activities to use with learners. There are five units at each level – E1, E2, E3, L1 and L2 – with teachers' notes which explain the rationale behind particular spelling strategies. See: **http://www.dfes.gov.uk/readwriteplus**

The Adult Literacy Core Curriculum (Basic Skills Agency, 2001) has useful boxes with advice on spelling, grammar and punctuation in the 'Writing' section.

See: **http://www.standards.dfes.gov.uk** – search for 'Language across the curriculum', Training Pack. See section on 'Spelling and Vocabulary'.

DVD: 'Spelling to learn: Using a learning styles approach to spelling with dyslexic learners', from LLU+, London South Bank University.

Look out for a new edition of *The Spelling Pack* from the Basic Skills Agency at NIACE. See: **http://www.basic–skills.co.uk**

7 Collaborative writing

We often think of writing as a solitary or individual activity, but it is useful to reflect how frequently writing is in fact a collaborative exercise. By the time this book goes to print many people will have contributed to the text, shaping the ideas and advising on, checking and correcting the presentation of these. At work it is usual for letters, reports and publicity, for example, to be the product of several people's efforts with texts sometimes circulating many times before a final version is agreed.

Collaboration can also happen at home, when family members or friends provide help, for example with an application form or difficult letter. One learner we interviewed explained how he managed his duties as chairman of a local museum.

> He explained how he drafts the letters and then asks a colleague to vet them. He then rewrites them. 'One person sets it going then someone else can pick holes in it.' Before meetings he writes briefing notes for himself. After the meeting he uses these notes to help him write the minutes then asks a colleague to check them before they are circulated.

In the literature review we note a number of writers who believe collaboration should be part of the classroom writing experience. We attempted to test out the effectiveness of collaboration in the research study but the findings were somewhat contradictory and inconclusive. We found that:

- in interview many learners spoke very positively about working with other learners and working in small groups;
- the statistical analysis suggested a link between the use of collaboration in teaching writing and a decrease in confidence in writing at work or in a public place;
- although we observed learners working collaboratively on exercises, for example on a particular aspect of grammar, or on the planning of a piece of writing, we saw very few occasions when they actually drafted a text together.

A small project enabled us to explore the potential of collaborative writing further. Six practitioners introduced collaborative writing into their classes and recorded their own observations and those of the learners on the experience.

The majority of their learners responded positively. Their comments support the theory that writing together in this way shifts the emphasis from the weaknesses of the individual to the combined strengths of the group.

What I liked was working in pairs which meant there was two people to put their ideas across instead of having to think of something on your own.

It was good to discuss ideas together because you were more clear of your story.

It benefited me a great deal because in a group you are talking to each other and sharing ideas rather than working on your own.

Project findings

Writing collaboratively encouraged learners to value each other's knowledge and experience and learn from one another.

Learners:

■ shared vocabulary;

■ discussed technical aspects of language; and

■ shared thoughts on editing the text as they were writing it.

Writing collaboratively gave learners the confidence to take greater risks with their writing than when writing alone.

Writing collaboratively gave opportunity for immediate peer feedback. This appeared to be more empowering than teacher feedback and also helped learners to become more aware of the needs of the reader of the writing. It also made the activities more authentic.

Writing collaboratively helped learners to understand the value of the planning and drafting stages of writing.

There were other positive outcomes for learners. Writing collaboratively supported:

■ sharing of cross-cultural knowledge;

■ development of team-working skills;

■ development of interpersonal skills; and

■ understanding of learners' additional needs.

What I enjoyed most was when we were writing different word to find the best words to use

I found it amazing how much learner centred discussion there was about technical aspects of writing/language. I didn't ask or direct them to discuss these things.

For me the most significant difference between their individual and collaborative work was their willingness to take a risk with structures when working collaboratively.

What I enjoyed most was having a new person look and give their opinion.

You're more conscious who you are writing for.

The progress made by P in the structure of her writing is very encouraging... they discussed the use of paragraphs and when a new one should be started.

I understand paragraphs now... that I need an introduction, a middle and an end

The teacher's role

The teacher's role was crucial to the success of the collaborative writing activities. The teachers agreed that:

- planning for collaborative writing must take account of group dynamics;
- group size is important; pairs or threes seemed to work best;
- careful questioning can be important to support groups;
- teachers need to be able to step back and allow the groups to engage but they also need to know when it is necessary to intervene to support learning; and
- care is needed in preparing materials for the activities (see below).

All teachers shared the fact that they were going to try writing collaboratively with their learners in advance and asked for feedback from learners on the experience.

Materials for collaborative writing activities

The teachers noted that it was important to choose the right materials for collaborative writing activities. Some materials encouraged interaction and others did not. The following are examples of materials that were successful.

- *Cards.* Laminated cards that the learners could move around as they discussed the activity drew the learners together and encouraged them to try out and discuss different arrangements. The teachers noted that when similar activities were undertaken using worksheets, learners tended to complete these individually and were less likely to make changes or discuss alternatives.
- *Drag and drop, computer-based activity.* A sequencing activity on a computer which required learners to drag and drop pictures also encouraged discussion of alternatives.
- *Pictures.* Carefully chosen pictures shared by the group provided a stimulus for writing but also encouraged discussion and questioning between learners. In one activity the teacher modelled the questions that learners might ask about a picture.
- *Large pieces of paper.* Two learners worked together on planning a piece of writing using an A3 sheet of paper. The size of the paper encouraged both learners to write on the sheet and provided scope for expansion of ideas.

Materials that are attractive and well produced encourage learners to respond positively to activities.

Reflect

It is worth stopping to think about your own writing practices. In what situations do you write collaboratively and what are the benefits and disadvantages?

Do we sometimes make writing more difficult for learners by assuming that writing should be an individual activity?

8 | Where next?

The preceding section illustrates how small action research projects undertaken by teachers in their own classrooms can provide valuable insights, for the teacher and the learners involved and for a wider audience. Throughout we have included prompts to encourage reflection and in conclusion we offer a list of suggestions for your own classroom research. We hope that, as well as providing a summary of the main messages in the guide, these will provide a stimulus for ongoing exploration of the teaching and learning of writing.

"The only way to learn how to write is to write."

Some of the suggestions below may involve taking risks. You may feel unsure how your learners will respond or uncertain about achieving the planned outcomes for your course. For teachers working in England they may challenge you to use the Core Curriculum for Adult Literacy in more holistic and imaginative ways. However, the experience of the teachers who took part in the project on collaborative writing suggest that taking risks can be worthwhile and that when learners are included as participants rather than as subjects in the research they can respond in surprising and positive ways.

- *Start with meaning.* If you usually make use of a lot of worksheet exercises to teach writing, introduce your learners to a number of activities that focus on what the writer has to say. Use the suggestions in Section 3 to support less able writers. Ask for feedback on these activities from your learners.

- *Support the process of writing.* Design an activity to check your learners' understanding of writing as a process. Based on the findings from this activity, plan activities to model and support the stages of the process in which your learners are least confident. Encourage learners to use these strategies in further writing tasks. Evaluate the effect of these activities on learners' writing with the learners.

- *Allow time for writing.* Choose a writing task with your learners that will engage their interest. Double the time you would usually allow for a writing task. Allow time for talk about the topic, the purpose and the process. Encourage and support the learners to take time on all aspects of the process. Discuss the completed pieces with the learners and check what each learner thinks he or she has learned while engaged on this task.

■ *Make links between writing inside and outside the class.* Look at the activity on p. 39 and adapt this to suit a group of your learners. Record what you learn. Also, check with learners what they learnt from the activity. Use what you learn to plan more explicit links between the learners' uses of writing outside the class and their aspirations in relation to writing and the writing they undertake in class. Evaluate this approach with the learners.

■ *Make use of the 'teachable moment'.* Ask a colleague to observe you responding to a learner's writing in class or ask a few learners if you can record your conversations with them about their work. Take copies of the writing and analyse these later (see pp. 50–51). Would you change the way you responded in the light of your analysis?

■ Introduce your learners to collaborative writing. Taking note of the findings reported in Section 7, plan activities that encourage your learners to work together on a piece of writing. Take time to observe your learners as they work together and record what you observe. Talk with your learners about their experience of the activities.

The only way to learn to write is to write. (Teeters, 1998)

References

Appleby, Y and Barton, D. (2007) *Responding to People's Lives*. Leicester: NIACE.

Basic Skills Agency (2001) *Adult Literacy Core Curriculum*. London: Basic Skills Agency. Available at **http://dfes.gov.uk/curriculum/literacy**

Bynner, J. and Parsons, S. (2006) *New Light on Literacy and Numeracy*. London: NRDC.

Casey, H., Jupp, T., Grief, S. Hodge, R., Ivanič, R., Lopez, D., Cara, O., Eldred, J. and McNeil, B. (2006) *You Wouldn't Expect a Maths Teacher to Teach Plastering. Embedding Literacy, Language and Numeracy in Post-16 Vocational Programmes – The Impact on Learning and Achievement*. London: NRDC.

CBI (2006) *Working on the 3 R's: Employers' Priorities for Functional Skills in Maths and English*. Sponsored by The Department for Education and Skills.

Condelli, L., Wrigley, H.,Yoon, K., Seburn, M., and Cronen, S. (2003) *What Works Study for Adult ESL Literacy Students*. Washington, DC: US Department of Education.

Crowther, J., Hamilton, M. and Tett, L. (2001) *Powerful Literacies*, Leicester: NIACE.

DfES (2005) *Skills for Life Learning Materials*. London: Department for Education and Skills.

Frank, A. (1954) *The Diary of Anne Frank*. London: Pan Books.

Gillespie, M. K. (1999) *Using Research on Writing, Focus on Basics*, Volume 3, Issue D, December 1999. National Center for the Study of Learning and Literacy. USA.

Grief, S., Kelly, S. and Soundranayagam, L. (2004) *Effective Approaches to the Teaching and Learning of Writing*. London: NRDC.

Grief, S., Meyer, B. and Burgess, A. (2007) *Effective Teaching and Learning*: Writing. London: NRDC.

Hedge, T. (1992) *Writing*. London: Oxford University Press.

Howard, U. (2006) 'Voices on the Page', *Basic Skills Bulletin*, 47.

Hyland, K. (2002) *Teaching and Researching Writing*. Pearson Education.

Ivanič R., Appleby, Y., Hodge, R., Trusting, K. and Barton, D. (2006) *Linking Learning and Everyday Life: A Social Perspective on Adult Language, Literacy and Numeracy Classes.* London: NRDC.

Jin, M. (1986) *Gifts from my Grandmother.* Sheba.

Kelly, S., Soundranayagam, L. and Grief, S. (2004) *Teaching and Learning Writing: A Review of Research and Practice.* London: NRDC.

McNamara. M. (2007) *Getting Better.* Gatehouse Media.

Mellar, H., Kambouri, M., Logan, K., Betts, S., Nance, B. and Moriarty, V. (2007) *Effective Teaching and Learning: Using ICT.* London: NRDC.

Mace, J. (2004) 'Language Experience: What's going on?', *Literacy Today*, 39.

Mace, J. (2005) 'Reflections on writing', *Reflect*, 4. NRDC.

Minton, C. (2004) *Report Writing at Work.* Suffolk County Council, Training Matters. Available from Avanti Books: **http://www.avantibooks.com**

Nance, B., Kambouri, M. and Mellar, H. (2007) *Using ICT. Developing Adult Teaching and Learning: Practitioner Guides.* Leicester: NIACE.

Petty, G. (2006) *Evidence-Based Teaching: A Practical Approach.* Cheltenham: Nelson Thornes.

Pullman, P. (2002) 'Give them a taste of honey', *Times Educational Supplement*, 8 February 2002.

Shaughnessy, M. P. (1977) *Errors and Expectations.* A Guide for the Teacher of Basic Writing. Oxford University Press.

Skills for Life Quality Initiative (2006) *Working with Young Adults*, research report. London: NRDC.

Spiegel, M. and Sunderland, H. (2006) *Teaching Basic Literacy to ESOL Learners.* LLU+, London South Bank University.

Teeters, P., (1998) *You Can Get Published.* Cincinnati: Writer's Digest Books.